SMALL PLAYS
FOR
SPECIAL DAYS

SMALL PLAYS FOR SPECIAL DAYS

BY SUE ALEXANDER
ILLUSTRATED BY TOM HUFFMAN

CLARION BOOKS
New York

For
Sherri and Keri Dearborn
Carin and Cindy Rosenberg
Pat and Tony Pollock
and
Jessica Meyers

Clarion Books
a Houghton Mifflin Company imprint
215 Park Avenue South, New York, NY 10003
Text copyright © 1977 by Sue Alexander
Illustrations copyright © 1977 by Tom Huffman

For information about permission to reproduce
selections from this book, write to Permissions,
Houghton Mifflin Company,
215 Park Avenue South, New York, NY 10003.

Printed in the USA

Library of Congress Cataloging-in-Publication Data

Alexander, Sue. Small plays for special days.
Bibliography.
Summary: Seven short plays for two actors about popular holidays with staging
notes and costume suggestions.
1. Holidays—Juvenile literature. [1. Holidays—Drama. 2. Plays]
I. Huffman, Tom.   II. Title.
PN6120.H7A55 812.5'4   76-28424   ISBN 0-618-38145-7   PA ISBN 0-618-37834-0

WOZ 20 19 18 17 16 15 14 13 12

CONTENTS

A NOTE ABOUT THIS BOOK

"Let's pretend" may be the most often repeated words of children at play. Imagination enables them to be another person, a scary ghost, or a shaggy lion without self-consciousness. At first this pretending is solitary play; then it begins to include a friend.

The plays—or skits—in this book, each containing just two characters, are extensions of this kind of play; an introduction to directed play-acting. With easily obtainable props, a minimum of costuming, actions and stage directions that require no special training to understand, children can make the transition from the easy informality of "let's pretend" to the more formalized role-playing of staged productions at school, recreation centers, or church.

This group of plays focuses on special days—holidays. As with any new activity, one element that is completely familiar, like a holiday, builds confidence in the child who has never before "pretended" in front of an audience. Though the themes are more contemporary than traditional, children will recognize and identify with the feelings and actions of the characters, enlarging their view of the world around them.

TO THE PLAYERS

Here are some holiday plays that you and a friend can do all by yourselves. They are fun to do, and easy, too. You can take turns being each of the different characters. You can be a Halloween ghost, a giant who wants a valentine, or a band leader on the Fourth of July. But you do not need to wait for the holidays to do the plays. You can do them anytime—anywhere.

Maybe you and your friend will want to act out the plays just for each other at home. The things you will need are all in your house. Maybe you will want to act them out for your class at school. If the things that you need are not in your classroom, think of other things you can use instead.

When you have acted out the plays once or twice, you may think of something else the ghost, the giant, or the band leader should say or do. The next time you act out the play —say it! And do it!

After you have acted out all the plays, you may want to make up some holiday plays of your own. You may think of other characters or other holidays. That is part of the fun of plays, too.

Now let the plays begin!

CHARACTERS

A Ghost
A Girl (or Boy)

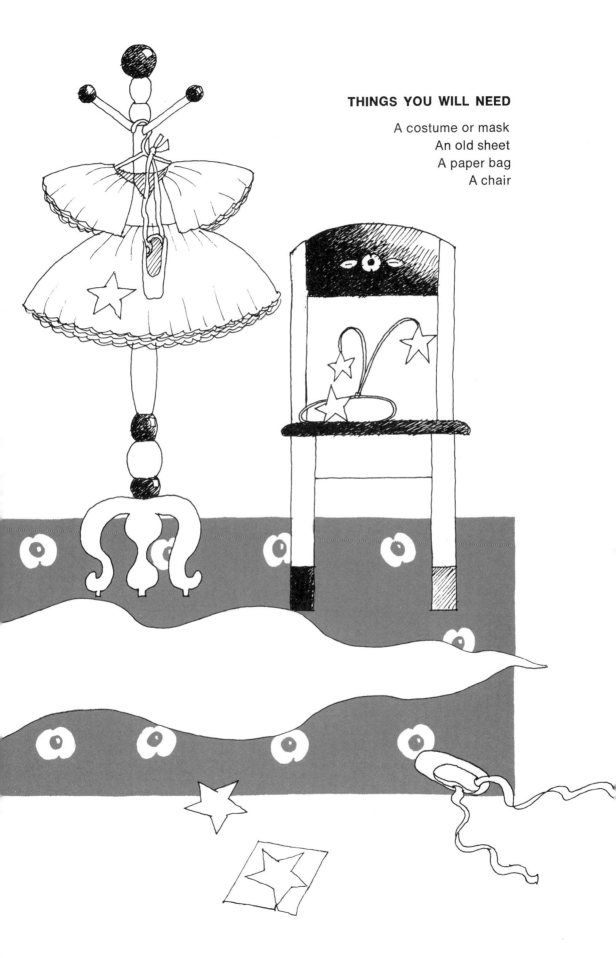

THINGS YOU WILL NEED

A costume or mask
An old sheet
A paper bag
A chair

THE PLAY BEGINS

The girl is walking down a dark street. She is carrying the Trick or Treat bag. She does not see the ghost hiding behind a bush (the chair).

GHOST   Oh, dear. Halloween is almost over and I haven't scared ANYONE!

He looks around the bush. He sees the girl.

Here comes a girl. I'll scare her!

GIRL   Oh, my. It's very dark on this street.

She walks past the bush.

GHOST   (softly) Ooo-ooo-ooh!

GIRL   What was THAT?

She stops and looks around. She does not see the ghost, so she keeps on walking.

GHOST   (a little louder) Ooo-ooo-ooh! Ooo-ooo-ooh!

GIRL   There it goes again!

She stops and looks around. She still does not see the ghost.

GHOST   (loud) Ooo-ooo-ooh! Ooo-ooo-ooh! Ooo-ooo-ooh!

He stands up very slowly. He rocks from side to side. The girl sees him.

GIRL   Oh, hello.

GHOST   HELLO! Is that all? Aren't you scared?

GIRL   Not really.

GHOST	But I'm a GHOST! Can't you tell?
GIRL	Well, you sound like a ghost. And you look like a ghost. But I'm not sure you ARE a ghost. Ghosts are supposed to DO scary things.
GHOST	I AM a ghost! I *do* do scary things!
GIRL	Like what?

The ghost comes out from behind the bush.

GHOST	Hmmm.

He stops. He thinks for a second.

How about a ghostly laugh? Like this: (very loud) HO, HO, HA, HA, HEE, HEE!

The girl shakes her head.

GIRL	That's not very scary. You sound like a broken record.
GHOST	Didn't it scare you even a little?
GIRL	No. You'll have to do something scarier than that.

GHOST   Hmmm. Let me think.

He walks back and forth. Then he stops.

I know what will scare you. I'll float!

He stands on tiptoes and flaps his arms. He goes all around the girl.

GHOST   There! Isn't that scary?

GIRL   Not really. I've seen scarier things on T.V.

GHOST   On T.V.! Oh, no!

GIRL   Well, goodbye, whoever you are.

She starts to walk away.

GHOST   Wait! I'll do something else. It will be the scariest thing you've ever seen. It will prove I'm a real ghost.

The girl stops.

GIRL   Well, all right. I'll give you just one more chance to prove you're a real ghost. What are you going to do?

The ghost is very excited. He flaps his arms. He comes very close to the girl.

GHOST   I'm going to make your Trick or Treat candy disappear!

He grabs the bag.

GIRL   Oh, no you won't!

The girl pulls the bag away from the ghost.

Now I'M going to do something scary!

The ghost is surprised.

GHOST   YOU are?

GIRL   Yes, I'm going to make YOU disappear!

She begins to chase the ghost.

GHOST   Oh! Help!

He runs behind the chair. The girl runs after him.

GIRL   HA, HA, HO, HO, HEE, HEE! Ooo-ooo-ooh!
Ooo-ooo-ooh! Ooo-ooo-ooh!

And the ghost runs off with the girl chasing him.

CHARACTERS

A Cat
A Dog

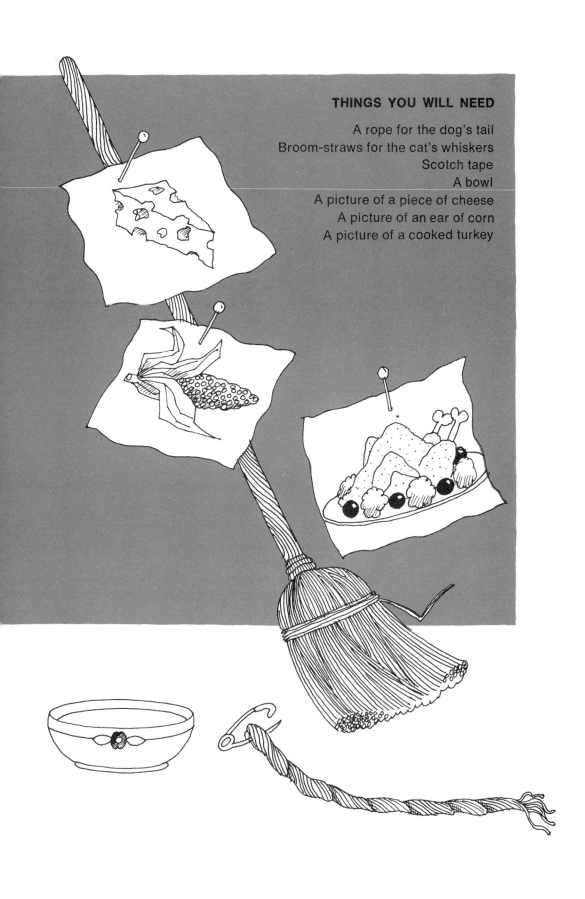

THINGS YOU WILL NEED

A rope for the dog's tail
Broom-straws for the cat's whiskers
Scotch tape
A bowl
A picture of a piece of cheese
A picture of an ear of corn
A picture of a cooked turkey

THE PLAY BEGINS

The cat is walking down the street very slowly. She is feeling sad. The dog comes along.

DOG Arf! Hello, Cat. You look sad. What's the matter?

The cat stops walking.

CAT Meow! Hello, Dog. I AM sad. The people in my house are getting ready for Thanksgiving. And they have no time for me.

DOG I know what you mean, Cat. That is what is happening where I live, too.

They walk along together. Then the dog stops.

Arf! Arf! Cat! Stop! I have a great idea!

The cat stops. She looks at the dog.

CAT What is it, Dog?

The dog is excited. He jumps up and down.

DOG You and I will celebrate Thanksgiving, too!

The cat gets excited. She jumps up and down.

CAT **ME-OW! That IS a good idea, Dog!**

Then the cat stops jumping. She looks sad again.

But how?

DOG **Let me think.**

He walks back and forth. The cat watches him. Then the dog stops.

Hmmm. I think that, first, we ought to get something to eat. My people are busy cooking today.

CAT **That sounds right, Dog. My people are cooking, too.**

The cat wiggles her whiskers.

I know! I will get some milk!

DOG **And I will find some cheese. Then we can share them!**

The cat jumps up and down.

CAT **This will be fun, Dog!**

DOG **I think so, too. All right, Cat. You get the milk. I will get the cheese. Then we will meet back here.**

CAT **Meow!**

The cat goes out. So does the dog. The cat comes back with the bowl. The dog comes back with the cheese.

DOG **That milk looks very tasty, Cat.**

CAT **So does the cheese, Dog.**

They pretend to eat. Then they exchange with each other.

I'm beginning to feel better, Dog. But it still doesn't feel quite like Thanksgiving.

DOG   Hmmm. You're right, Cat.

He thinks for a minute.

I know! We need some songs to sing. Do you know any songs?

CAT   Of course.

DOG   Then let's sing, Cat!

The cat and dog hold hands. Then they begin to sing.

CAT   ME-oww! Me-OWWW! MEEE-OWWWW!

DOG   Arf! ARF! Arf-ARF-arf! ARF!

CAT   That was nice, Dog. You sing very well.

DOG   Thank you, Cat. You do too.

The cat looks sad again. She sits down and whimpers.

Now what's the matter, Cat?

CAT   Meow! Dog, we are still missing something.

DOG   What?

CAT   I'm not sure. But I know that SOMETHING is still not right.

The cat whimpers again.

DOG   Don't cry, Cat. I'll go see if I can find what we are missing.

The dog goes off and comes back with the ear of corn. He puts it down in front of the cat.

Does this make our Thanksgiving right, Cat?

CAT   Meow! No, Dog. That isn't what we are missing. Besides, I don't even LIKE corn.

DOG   Come to think of it, neither do I.

CAT   Meow! Meow! Oh, dear! Meow!

DOG   Do stop crying, Cat. I'll try again.

The dog goes off and comes back with the turkey. He puts it down in front of the cat.

This will make it right, Cat! Almost everyone has turkey for Thanksgiving!

CAT   That's true, Dog. And I do like turkey. But . . .

DOG   But what?

CAT   But that's not what is missing! Meow!

DOG   Listen, Cat. We have milk and cheese. We have songs to sing. We even have turkey! What else is there?

CAT   Meow! FAMILY! That's what!

DOG   FAMILY?

CAT   Yes. My people have grandparents and aunts and uncles. They have cousins, too. And they all get together at Thanksgiving time!

The cat begins to cry very loud.

Meow-meow-meow!

DOG   Please stop crying, Cat. Let me think.

He walks back and forth. Then he stops. He jumps up and down. He is very excited.

Cat, listen! My people haven't any grandparents. They haven't any aunts, uncles or cousins. But they DO have family on Thanksgiving! And we will too!

CAT   How, Dog?

DOG   The same way my people do! With good friends! Arf! I will be your family! And you will be mine!

CAT   Oh, Dog! You are so smart! Now our Thanksgiving will be just right! Let's sing some more!

DOG   Sing a song of happy times
Good friends are near

CAT   Sing a song of happy times
Thanksgiving's here!

And they go out singing and saying "meow" and "arf."

24

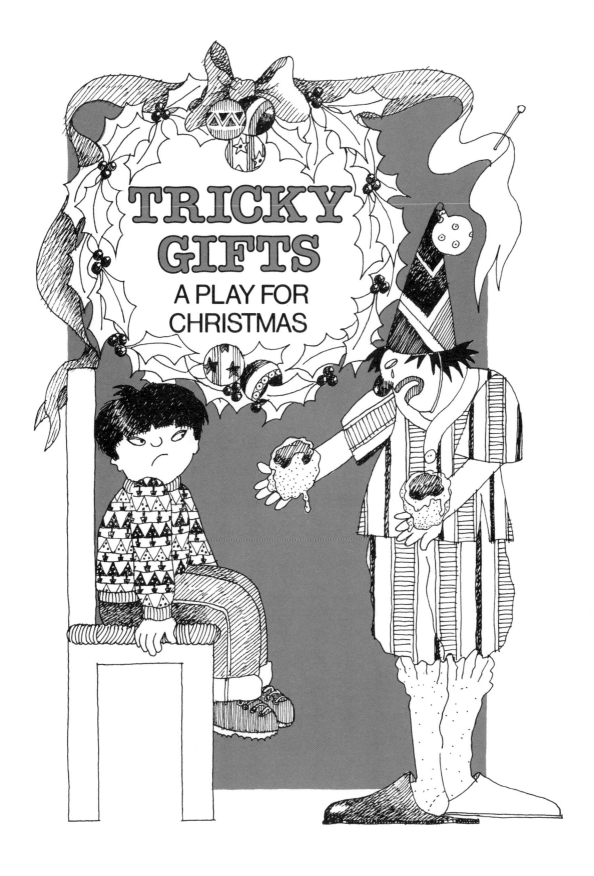

TRICKY GIFTS

A PLAY FOR CHRISTMAS

CHARACTERS

A Circus Clown
A Boy (or Girl)

THINGS YOU WILL NEED

A chair
A table
A hat
Water-paint for the clown's nose
Two small balls
A pot and spoon
Some clay

THE PLAY BEGINS

The clown is practicing his act. The boy comes in and sits down on the chair to watch. The clown does a somersault. Then he pretends to sit on an invisible chair—and falls down. The boy claps. The clown stands up.

CLOWN   Oh, dear!

BOY   What's wrong, Clown? Your act looks fine to me.

CLOWN   That's not what is bothering me. Tomorrow is Christmas and I haven't anything to give my family!

BOY   Oh, my. That's too bad.

CLOWN   I don't want to think about it. It makes me too sad. I'll practice my act some more.

He goes out and gets the two balls. He comes back and juggles them.

BOY   Clown! I've just thought of something!

He jumps up from the chair.

Maybe you can *make* your Christmas gifts!

The clown stops juggling the balls.

CLOWN   That sounds like a good idea! Now what can I make?

He walks back and forth, juggling the balls while he is thinking. Then he stops.

I know! I will make some bowls!

BOY   Bowls do make nice gifts.

The clown puts the balls on the table and runs out.
He comes back with the clay.

CLOWN   These will be beautiful bowls!

He starts to mold the clay, but he doesn't do it
very well.

BOY   Um . . . Clown, are you sure you know how to
make bowls? That doesn't look like a very good
bowl.

The clown holds it up and looks at it.

CLOWN   Oh, dear. You're right. It's a TERRIBLE bowl!

He puts it down. Then he starts to cry.

BOY   Don't cry, Clown. Perhaps we can think of
something else for you to make.

The boy walks back and forth while he is thinking.

I have an idea!

He stops.

Clown, why don't you make some candy?
Everyone likes candy!

CLOWN   That's a good idea! I'll go get it started!

He runs off. He comes back with the pot and the
spoon.

There! Everything is in the pot. Now all I have
to do is stir it until it gets hard.

He stirs the spoon in the pot.

BOY	How long is it supposed to take?
CLOWN	Oh, just a minute or two.

He stirs and stirs and stirs.

That's funny. It doesn't seem to be getting hard at all.

BOY	Let me see it.

He goes and looks in the pot.

Clown, that's the strangest looking candy I've ever seen!

The clown looks in the pot.

CLOWN	You're right! It does look strange! And it's not getting hard at all! Oh, dear!

He puts the pot on the table. Then he cries louder than he did before.

It's no use! I can't make bowls. And I can't make candy. I can't make anything!

BOY	Calm down, Clown. We will think of something.

The boy goes back to the chair and sits down. He thinks for a second.

There has to be SOMETHING you can make . . .

Then he looks at the balls and at the clown. He jumps up, very excited.

There is!

CLOWN	What?
BOY	You can make people LAUGH!

30

CLOWN	Of course I can. That's my job. But what does it have to do with Christmas gifts?

The boy picks up the balls. He jumps up and down.

BOY	You can give gifts of laughter! Do a trick for everyone on your list!

He hands the balls to the clown.

CLOWN	Do you really think that's a good gift?
BOY	Yes! It's the best kind!
CLOWN	Then I'll do it!

He jumps up and down. He is very happy.

Let's see. I'll juggle for Uncle Jim.

He juggles the balls.

I'll do a somersault for Aunt Mary.

He puts the balls down. Then he does a somersault.

And I'll sit on my invisible chair for Cousin Bob!

He sits on air—and falls down. The boy claps very loud.

BOY	Those are wonderful tricks, Clown! I wish I could do them.

The clown jumps up. He pulls the boy from the chair.

CLOWN	I'll teach you! Then we'll all have a Merry Christmas!
BOY	Hooray!

And they both somersault off.

the cat ate

$2 + 2 = 4$

$2 \times 2 = 4$

GIANT

FOR OGRE

FOR GIANT

THINGS YOU WILL NEED

Two chairs
A banner with the word GIANT on it
A picture of an eye
Scotch tape
Two valentines
A sign with the words FOR GIANT
A sign with the words FOR OGRE

THE PLAY BEGINS

The giant is sitting on a rock (a chair) in the forest. Her friend, the ogre, comes along.

OGRE   **ARRGH! Good day, Giant. My goodness, you look sad!**

GIANT   **Good day to you, Ogre. You don't look very happy yourself.**

The ogre sits down on the other rock.

OGRE   **ARRGH! You're right, Giant. I am not very happy. Today is Valentine's Day. And no one has sent me a valentine.**

He rubs the eye on his forehead.

GIANT   **That's my trouble, too, Ogre.**

She gets up and takes giant-steps back and forth.

Why do you suppose we didn't get any, Ogre?

OGRE   **ARRGH! I don't know.**

He thinks for a minute.

Unless it's because we have eaten most of the people in the neighborhood.

He licks his lips.

GIANT   **Hmmm. That might be the reason.**

She sits down again.

Still, you would think that there was ONE person left who would send us a valentine!

They both sit and look sad. Then the ogre smiles. He has thought of something.

OGRE   I have to go now. I just remembered something I have to do. Goodbye.

He gets up and goes out.

GIANT   I have an idea! I will get Ogre a valentine!

She gets up and runs out. The ogre comes back in. He is carrying a valentine and the sign that says "For Giant."

OGRE   ARRGH! Good! Giant is not here. I can surprise her! I have a valentine for her! I will put it on her rock. Then I will hide!

He puts the valentine on the giant's rock. Then he goes behind his rock and scrunches down. The giant comes in. She is carrying a valentine and the sign that says "For Ogre."

GIANT   Good! Ogre is not back yet. He will be very surprised.

She puts the valentine and the sign on the ogre's rock. Just then the ogre stands up.

OH! Hello, Ogre.

The Giant sees the sign on her rock.

Look, Ogre! Someone has left something for me!

She goes over and picks up the valentine. She opens it up.

Listen to this, Ogre. It says:
  "I love people, snakes and mice
    And they taste very fine
    But none are quite so nice
    As you—my VALENTINE!"
Oh, Ogre! It's from you! Thank you!

38

OGRE   You're welcome, Giant.

The ogre comes out from behind the rock.

Oh! Someone has left something for me, too!

He picks up the valentine on his rock and opens it up.

It's a valentine! It says:
   "Fee, Fie, Fo and Fum
     Today I'm going to eat someone
     These are favorite words of mine
     And they're for you—my VALENTINE."
And it's from you! Oh, Giant, I feel much better!

GIANT   This has turned out to be a good day, after all!

OGRE   Yes. But the valentines have made me hungry. I think I will go find someone sweet to eat.

He licks his lips.

GIANT   That sounds good. I'll go with you!

They go out together.

40

ROAR!
SAID THE LION

A PLAY FOR
THE FIRST DAY OF SPRING

CHARACTERS

A Lion
A Lamb

A paper collar for the lion's mane
Cotton for the lamb's ears and tail
A chair
A picture of lilies
A picture of strawberries

THE PLAY BEGINS

The lamb is skipping through the forest. She is very happy.

LAMB   I love Spring! Everything smells so good!

The lion runs in.

LION   ROAR! Here I come, Lamb! I'm going to eat you! ROAR!

The lamb stops and looks at the lion.

LAMB   If you say so, Lion. But before you eat me, let me show you something.

LION   ROAR!

LAMB   Look, Lion. It is the beginning of Spring. And the lilies are beginning to blossom.

The lamb goes over to the lilies.

Aren't they pretty? They smell good, too.

LION   Yes, Lamb, they are pretty. And I know it is the beginning of Spring. But now I am going to eat you! ROAR!

He starts to run after the lamb. The lamb runs behind the tree (chair).

LAMB   Wait, Lion! I want to show you something else.

The lion stops. He looks disgusted.

LION   NOW what?

LAMB   Um-um-um. . . .

44

The lamb looks around for something to show the lion. Then she looks at the tree she is standing behind.

This tree! See, Lion, it has new buds. Soon we shall have green leaves. They will give us shade.

LION **Very nice, Lamb. I do like to rest in the shade after a good meal. But now I am going to eat you! ROAR!**

He begins to run behind the tree. The lamb scrunches down.

LAMB **I suppose you must, Lion. But there _is_ one more thing I would like to show you.**

LION **ROAR! I am losing my temper, Lamb! ROAR!**

LAMB **It's too beautiful a day to lose your temper, Lion. Do stop roaring. Besides, how can you eat me if you are roaring?**

LION **Hmmm.**

He thinks for a second.

That's true, Lamb. Very well. I will let you show me one more thing. But just ONE! And then I AM going to eat you!

LAMB **All right, Lion. If you must, you must.**

The lamb comes out from behind the tree, making sure to walk far away from the lion. She goes over to the strawberries.

Over here. This is what I wanted to show you.

LION **What is it?**

LAMB **Wild strawberries. The first ones of Spring.**

She picks one and eats it.

They're delicious!

LION   Hmmm. Move over, Lamb. I think I'll try one of those strawberries.

The lion comes over to the strawberries. The lamb runs back behind the tree. The lion eats a strawberry.

My! It is delicious! I think I'll have another.

He eats another one. Then he sits down and eats them all.

LAMB   My goodness, Lion! You have eaten all the strawberries!

The lion looks up.

LION   Hmmm. So I have.

He starts to get up. Then he sits down again.

Oooh! Oh! Oooh!

He puts his hands on his stomach.

LAMB   What's the matter, Lion?

LION   I have a terrible stomach ache! I must have eaten too many strawberries! Oooh! Oh! Oooh!

The lion gets up and starts to run off.

LAMB   Why, Lion, are you going somewhere?

LION   Yes! I'm going HOME! Oooh! Oh! Oooh!

LAMB   Home! Does that mean you're not going to eat me?

The lion stops and looks at the lamb. He is disgusted.

LION   EAT you! I'm not even going to TALK to you! It's your fault I have this terrible stomach ache! Oooh! Oh! Oooh!

He rubs his stomach. Then he runs a bit further.

LAMB   Well, Lion, have a good trip home. And if anyone asks me what I liked best about the first day of Spring—I'll say, "Watching Lion make a PIG of himself!" Goodbye!

The lamb runs off.

LION   Oooh! Oh! Oooh!

The lion rubs his stomach and runs off the other way.

CHARACTERS
A Boy (or Girl)
A Father (or Mother)

THINGS YOU WILL NEED

A book
A chair
A picture of a gorilla
A picture of a snake
A picture of a seal

TALES
OF
ODIOUS
HORROR

THE PLAY BEGINS

The father is sitting in a chair in his living room. He is reading the book. The boy comes running in.

BOY   Father! Come quick! There's a gorilla in my room!

The father looks up from his book.

FATHER   Don't be silly. That's an April Fool's joke. Of course there is no gorilla in your room!

He reads his book again.

BOY   But, Father, the gorilla is jumping up and down—like this!

The boy jumps up and down and scratches himself as a gorilla would.

FATHER   I must say, you make a very good gorilla! But now I want to read my book. Go into your room and find something to do.

The boy goes out slowly. He runs back in.

BOY   Father! Now there's a snake in my room, too! He is wriggling around and saying HSSSSSS!

The father puts down his book and stands up.

FATHER   That's enough! First you tell me that there is a gorilla in your room! That he is jumping around like this!

He jumps around like a gorilla.

52

Now you tell me there is a snake in your room! And he is saying HSSSS! Those are just silly stories! And I want to read my book. Go to your room!

The boy goes out slowly. The father sits down and reads his book again. The boy runs back in.

BOY   Father! PLEASE come quick! Now there is a seal in my room! And he is saying GWARK! And he is clapping his fins together—like this!

The boy bounces like a seal and claps his hands.

GWARK! GWARK!

FATHER   Hmmm. Maybe I had better go and look after all. If those animals ARE in your room, we will have to call the zoo!

He puts down his book and gets up and goes out.

BOY   Ha! Ha! I did it! I made him look! And there's nothing there! What a good April Fool's joke!

The father runs back in, very excited.

FATHER   You were right! There IS a seal in your room! And a snake! And a gorilla! AND THEY ARE ALL ON YOUR BED! We had better call the zoo!

The boy jumps up. He is very surprised at what his father has said.

BOY   WHAT? How can that be? I'd better go see!

He runs out. He comes back carrying the pictures of the seal, snake and gorilla. He is smiling.

FATHER   And a happy April Fool's Day to you, too!

They laugh and go off together.

CHARACTERS

A Band Leader
A Girl (or Boy)

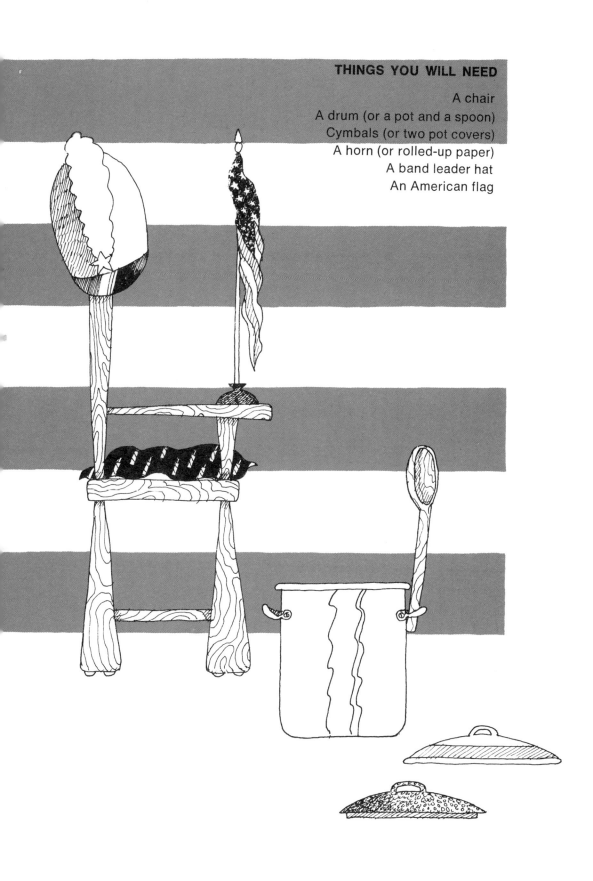

THINGS YOU WILL NEED

A chair
A drum (or a pot and a spoon)
Cymbals (or two pot covers)
A horn (or rolled-up paper)
A band leader hat
An American flag

THE PLAY BEGINS

The band leader is sitting on the chair. The girl comes in.

LEADER   **So you want to be in the Fourth of July parade. Are you a good musician?**

GIRL   **Oh, yes! I'll show you!**

She goes out and comes back with the drum.

One-two-three . . .

She bangs the drum.

One-two-three . . .

She bangs the drum again.

LEADER   **Stop!**

He stands up and holds up his hands.

You are not a good drum player at all!

The girl looks sad. She puts down her drum.

GIRL   **Oh, dear! I want so much to be in the parade!**

She starts to cry. She rubs her eyes.

LEADER   **Don't cry! Tears make me nervous!**

He sits down.

Maybe you can do something else. Do you play any other instruments?

The girl stops crying.

GIRL   Yes! I play the cymbals! I'll show you.

She takes the drum out and comes back with the cymbals.

One-two-three . . .

She claps the cymbals together.

One-two-three . . .

She claps the cymbals again.

LEADER   STOP!

He jumps up. He puts his hands over his ears.

You play the cymbals worse than you play the drum!

GIRL   Oh, dear!

She thinks for a second.

Well, maybe you will like the way I play the horn. I'll get it!

She runs off with the cymbals and comes back with the horn.

Listen to this! One-two-three . . .

She blows the horn.

One-two-three . . .

She blows the horn again.

LEADER   Oh, no! Stop!

He jumps up.

PLEASE don't play any more! I can't stand it! You're the worst musician I ever heard!

GIRL   But I want to be in the parade!

She starts to cry.

LEADER   I told you before, tears make me nervous! Please stop crying!

GIRL   I can't!

She cries louder.

LEADER   There must be some way I can get you to stop crying!

He covers his ears.

If you don't stop crying, we won't have a Fourth of July parade—we'll have a Fourth of July FLOOD!

GIRL   You're making me feel worse!

She cries as loud as she can.

LEADER   I had better think of some way to stop those tears—and fast!

He gets up. He walks back and forth while he is thinking. Then he stops.

I have an idea! Do you know how to march?

The girl stops crying. She wipes her eyes.

GIRL Yes.

LEADER Hmmm. You had better show me.

The girl marches back and forth.

Very good! Wait here!

He runs out and comes back with the flag.

Do you think you can march and wave the flag at the same time?

GIRL Of course! That's easy!

LEADER Great! Oh! It's time for the parade to begin. Come on!

He starts to walk off.

GIRL You mean I get to be in the parade after all?

The leader stops.

LEADER You're not only going to be IN the parade— you're going to LEAD it!

He hands the girl the flag.

GIRL Hooray!

She jumps up and down.

LEADER Well, are you ready?

GIRL And how! Let's go!

She holds the flag up high.

One-two-three! One-two-three!

And she marches off waving the flag. The leader marches off behind her.

PLAYS FOR FURTHER PERFORMING

These plays have been chosen with the interests and abilities of children in mind, as well as the resources of elementary schools. Some of the books listed are out of print but may be available through a public library. Starred entries (*) indicate those plays that may be performed before a nonpaying audience without payment of royalty fees or permission from the copyright holder.

*Alexander, Sue. *Small Plays for You and a Friend* (New York: Clarion Books, 1974). Five original short plays designed specifically for two actors, with notes on staging and adapting the plays, including simple directions for the actors and a list of the props needed. Suitable for classroom production. Ages 6–9.

*Barchers, Suzanne I. *Readers Theatre for Beginning Readers* (Englewood, Colorado: Teacher Ideas Press, 1993). More than 20 folktales and fables ("Belling the Cat," "Three Billy Goats Gruff," "The Tortoise and the Hare," etc.) on reproducible script pages with specific suggestions for presentation, props, and delivery. Suitable for classroom production. Ages 6–9.

*Bruchac, Joseph. *Pushing Up the Sky: Seven Native American Plays for Children* (New York: Dial Books, 2000). Plays adapted from tales told by seven different tribes in North America (Zuni, Tlingit, Cherokee, etc.). Each play is prefaced by some information about the tribe and its locale. Staging, props, and costuming are discussed. Suitable for auditorium production. Ages 9 and up.

*Giff, Patricia Reilly. *Show Time at the Polk Street School* (New York: Dell Yearling, 1992). Three plays adapted from the Polk Street School books (*The Candy Corn Contest, The Secret at the Polk Street School, Fancy Feet*). Staging, props, costuming, and makeup are noted and discussed. Suitable for classroom or auditorium production. Ages 7–10.

*Korty, Carol. *Plays from African Folktales* (New York: Scribners, 1975). Four humorous plays emphasizing the use of pantomime. Simple costuming and props. The back of the book contains directions for adding music, dance, and African masks, if desired. Suitable for classroom production. Ages 8–12.

Marx, Pamela. *Take a Quick Bow!* (Illinois: Good Year Books, 1997). Twenty-six short plays and choral speaking performance pieces; some original, others based on existing material (i.e., Dickens's *A Christmas Carol,* Shakespeare's sonnets, Vivaldi's *The Four Seasons,* legends, folklore, etc.). Notes for teachers on staging, props, and costumes. Geared for classroom production. Ages 7–9.

Sendak, Maurice. Music by Carole King. *Really Rosie: Starring the Nutshell Kids* (New York: Harper & Row, 1975). Scenario of the television show, including the stories from the Nutshell books (*Chicken Soup with Rice, Pierre,* etc.); simple musical arrangements for guitar or piano. Costuming suggested by the illustrations. Suitable for classroom or auditorium production. Ages 7–12.

Plays: The Drama Magazine for Young People (Waukesha, Wisconsin: Kalmbach Publishing Company). Published monthly, October through May. Contains plays, skits, sketches, spotlights. Some suitable for classroom production. Ages 8–12 (and up).